Dinosaur Mazes

Patricia Wynne

Dover Publications, Inc.
New York

Published in Canada by General Publishing Company, Ltd., 30 Lesmill Road, Don Mills, Toronto, Ontario.
Published in the United Kingdom by Constable and Company, Ltd., 3 The Lanchesters, 162–164 Fulham Palace Road, London W6 9ER.

Dinosaur Mazes is a new work, first published by Dover Publications, Inc., in 1992.

International Standard Book Number: 0-486-27110-2

Manufactured in the United States of America
Dover Publications, Inc., 31 East 2nd Street, Mineola, N.Y. 11501

Introduction

The mighty dinosaurs walked the earth millions of years ago, but they still travel the winding paths in this collection of 46 dinosaur mazes. You'll find familiar favorites like *Triceratops*, *Stegosaurus* and *Apatosaurus*—and many creatures that might be new to you. Help these funny and ferocious monsters avoid pitfalls and dead ends to get to their goals. Danger may await you, but it's all part of the thrill of the twistings and turnings on the way.

Now you can aid *Tyrannosaurus* as he tries to catch a flying reptile, save *Indosaurus* from the lava and ash of an erupting volcano, and lead *Camarasaurus* safely to her baby through a pack of bloodthirsty *Allosaurus*. If you find any maze too tricky, you may turn to the section of solutions that begins on page 52. When you have completed the mazes, you can have even more fun by coloring in the pictures in this book with pencils, pens or crayons!

Help *Ornithomimus* catch a dragonfly for lunch.

FINISH

START

Acrocanthosaurus needs your help to find the trees.

Barosaurus has a long neck with which it can reach
the highest leaves. Show that this is true.

Can *Camarasaurus* get to her baby without being attacked by that pack of vicious *Allosaurus*?

START

FINISH

Corythosaurus is hungry—help him reach a plant that he can eat.

Can you find your way through this sail-spined *Spinosaurus*?

Guide this swimming *Anatosaurus* between the water plants to reach the shore (*at lower right*).

Lead *Rhamphorhynchus* on her flight to build a nest among the trees below.

FINISH

START

Ostrich-like *Struthiomimus* thinks that catching a frog is hard work. Show him how easy it is.

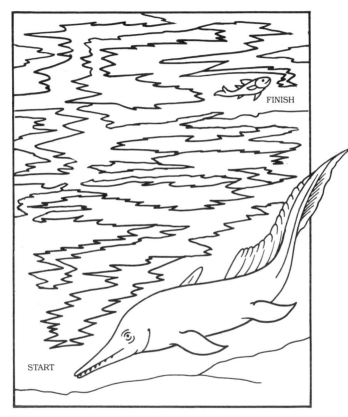

START

FINISH

Mixosaurus (*bottom*) likes fish for dinner, but this one might be too quick for her to catch.

13

Help *Pteranodon* glide to her waiting eggs below.

This *Indosaurus* must run quickly to get away from the active volcano that is spewing out hot ash and rock.

START

FINISH

The giant turtle, *Archelon*, needs more fish to grow even bigger.

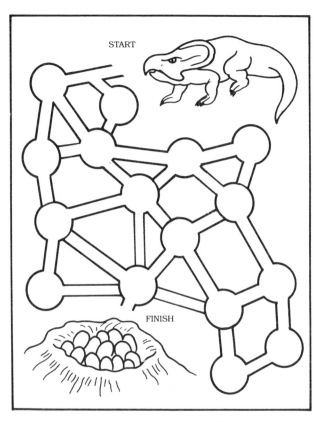

Guide *Protoceratops* along the path to her nest.

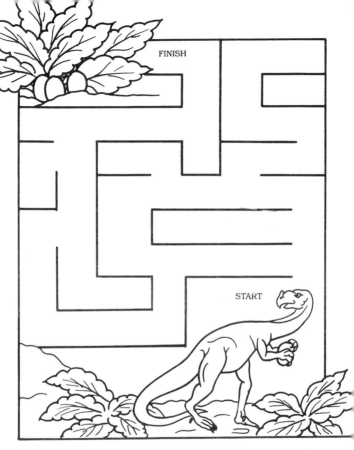

FINISH

START

The *Oviraptor* is still hungry—he would like another egg from the nest.

START

FINISH

Help this hippo-like *Lystrosaurus* find his way
down the stream to the plant.

FINISH

START

Can *Archaeopteryx*, one of the first birds, fly through the clouds to the treetops?

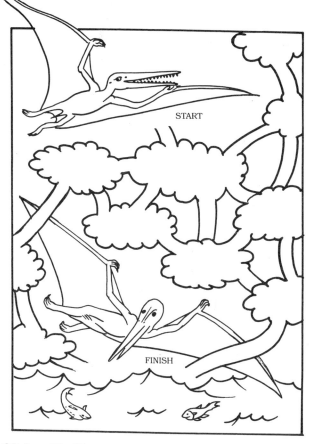

START

FINISH

Glide with *Pterosaurus* down to the sea to catch fish.

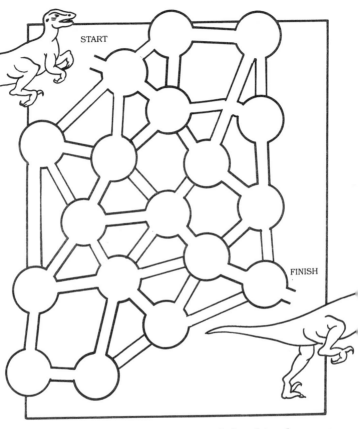

START

FINISH

Help *Deinonychus* catch up with his friend.

Lead *Alamosaurus* to the tasty plants growing on the cliff.

Help *Ankylosaurus* locate a good hiding place.

START

FINISH

An *Elasmosaurus* has swallowed a fish. Help the fish escape through that tooth-filled mouth.

25

START

FINISH

Lead *Styracosaurus* through these branches and make sure he eats only 14 leaves gathered from the circles.

26

Can you help *Leptoceratops* (*top right*) get through
the maze to pick flowers (*at the bottom*) without
being attacked by the two *Albertosaurus*?

FINISH

START

Protoceratops would like to join the pair at the top of the page.

28

Can the *Pachycephalosaurus* at the top get in touch with his friend at the bottom without getting into the fight?

This *Parasaurolophus* would like to snack on some delicious horsetails. Can you show him the way?

START

FINISH

One of these *Procompsognathus* would like to visit the other by the ferns. See if you can be any help.

Choose your path carefully and you will meet up with a gentle, plant-eating *Saurolophus*. Only one set of footprints will lead you to your goal.

Pteranodons don't like to get wet. Help this one fly out of the water and up to the clouds.

START

FINISH

Spinosaurus has gotten too hot in the sun. Lead him to the shade of a giant fern.

FINISH

START

This *Tyrannosaurus* leaps his way through the maze to catch the airborne *Quetzalcoatlus*. Will he succeed?

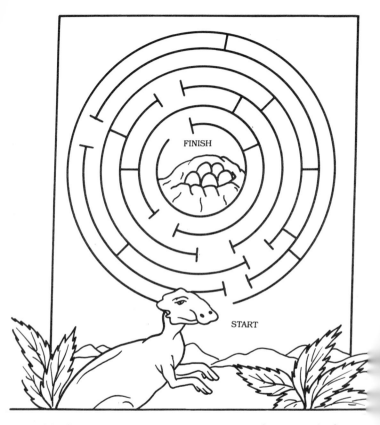

FINISH

START

Mother *Maiasaura* must return to her nest before her young break out of their shells.

The solitary *Compsognathus* would like to join her friends on the other side of the maze. See if you can make sure she gets there.

This daring *Dimorphodon* is trying to land on the edge of a cliff. Guide him through the clouds.

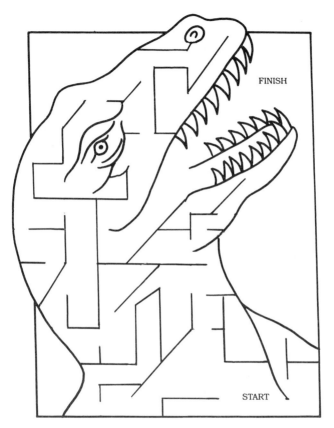

FINISH

START

Start in the throat of terrible *Tyrannosaurus* and work your way on out of his mouth. Watch those choppers!

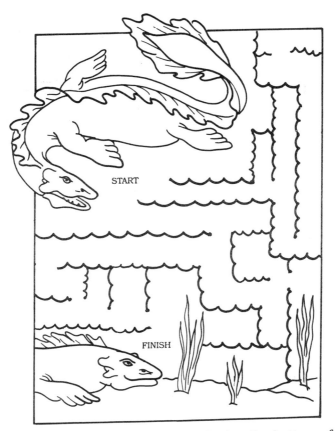

START

FINISH

Tylosaurus wants to look for food at the bottom of the sea. See that she gets there.

START

START

Iguanodons love to fight—but first they have to find
each other. Start from either end of the maze.

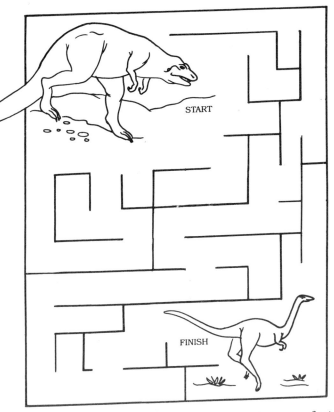

START

FINISH

The speedy, sleek *Struthiomimus* must run as fast as possible to escape the fierce *Megalosaurus*.

Help *Triceratops* find the rest of the herd.

START

FINISH

The *Stegosaurus* at the top of the page wants to join the other one for a nice leafy meal.

FINISH

START

Apatosaurus can pick the leaves from tall trees—if
you help him out!

45

START

FINISH

Pachycephalosaurus has a long way to go to get to the oasis—see if you can help.

Can the prehistoric fish *Aspidorhynchus* (*right*) get past the icthyosaur to the safety of his cave?

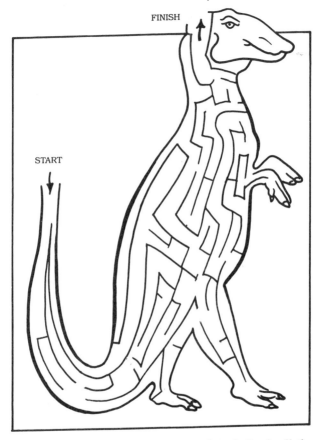

Enter *Trachodon* by way of his tail and climb all the way up to his head.

The *Ouranosaurus* (*right*) must get past this fear-some *Tyrannosaurus* to reach the horsetails and the water.

Solutions

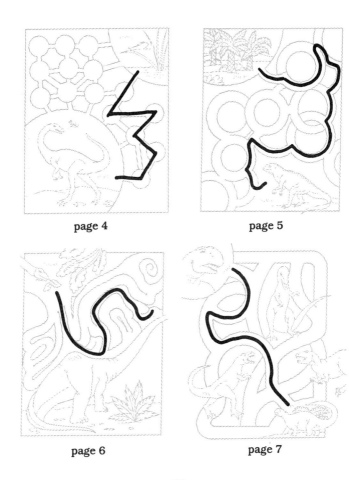

page 4

page 5

page 6

page 7

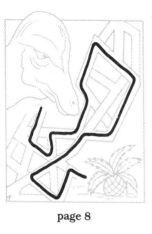

page 8

page 9

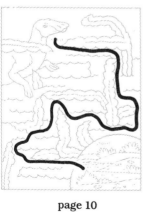

page 10

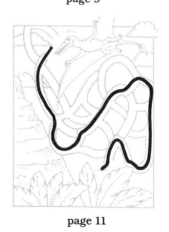

page 11

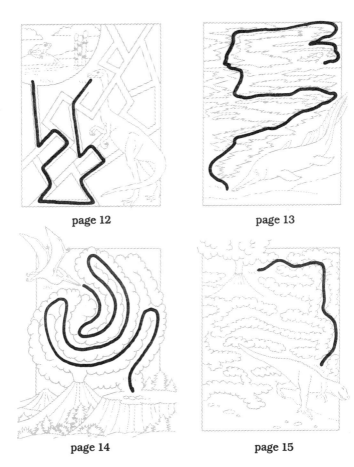

page 12

page 13

page 14

page 15

page 16

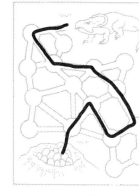

page 17

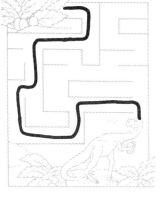

page 18

page 19

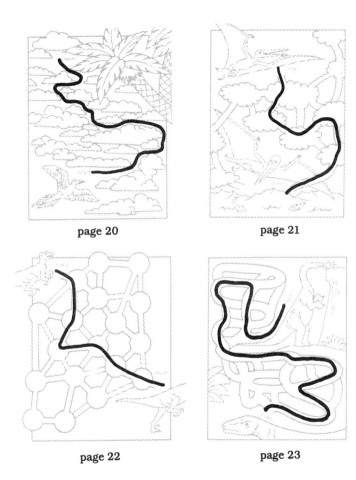

page 20

page 21

page 22

page 23

page 24

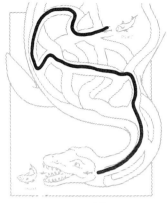

page 25

page 26

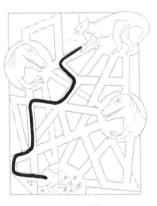

page 27

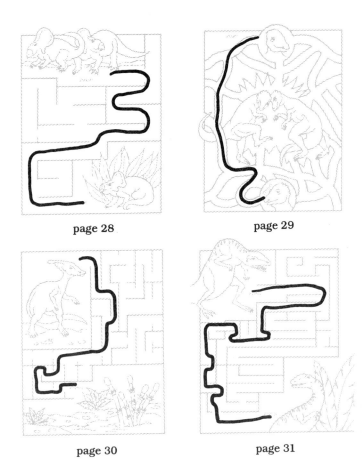

page 28

page 29

page 30

page 31

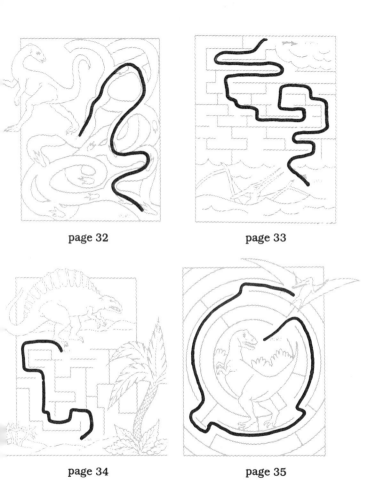

page 32

page 33

page 34

page 35

page 36

page 37

page 38

page 39

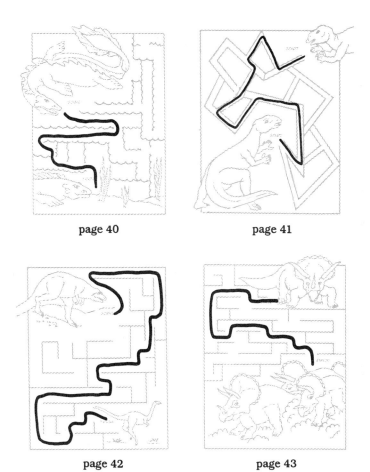

page 40

page 41

page 42

page 43

page 44

page 45

page 46

page 47

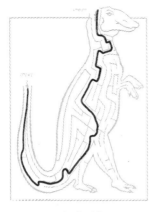

page 48

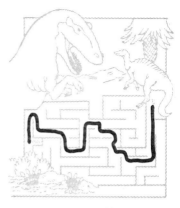

page 49